Follow the beautiful trail
   wherever God leads you...
He goes with you step by step
with open arms and heart;
trust Him on your journey,
for God is the maker of every dream
and the keeper of all His promises.

Linda E. Knight

When God
Puts a Dream
in Your Heart...
Anything Is Possible!

A Collection of Writings
About Having Faith
and Fulfilling Your Destiny

Edited by Gary Morris

Blue Mountain Press ™

Boulder, Colorado

Library of Congress Control Number: 2005905274
ISBN: 1-59842-064-X

ACKNOWLEDGMENTS appear on page 64.

Certain trademarks are used under license.
BLUE MOUNTAIN PRESS is registered in U.S. Patent and Trademark Office.

Printed in the United States of America.
First Printing: 2006

 This book is printed on recycled paper.

This book is printed on fine quality, laid embossed, 80 lb. paper. This paper has been specially produced to be acid free (neutral pH) and contains no groundwood or unbleached pulp. It conforms with all the requirements of the American National Standards Institute, Inc., so as to ensure that this book will last and be enjoyed by future generations.

Blue Mountain Arts, Inc.

P.O. Box 4549, Boulder, Colorado 80306

Contents

When God
Puts a Dream
in Your Heart...

Follow the beautiful trail
   wherever He leads you.
Be open to what each day asks of you
and welcome what it may hold,
knowing the desires of your heart
   are in God's hands.
No matter where life leads,
He goes with you step by step
with open arms and heart;
trust Him on your journey.
He is the maker of every dream
and the keeper of all His promises;
share in the joy of celebrating
   what He's given you.
Find joy in every opportunity
to live out His purpose for you,
and know your efforts have meaning.
Accept any detours as part of His plan;
keep your eyes on God
and you'll never lose your way.

Linda E. Knight

Just for Today... See Yourself the Same Way God Does

Wouldn't every day be wonderful if you could see yourself the same way God does? As a beautiful creation created for a specific purpose and plan; someone who is valued, cherished, seen as a wonderful treasure — and given a love so unconditional and perfect you can't even comprehend it.

You were designed by the hand of God. You may sometimes make mistakes or fall short of your expectations, dreams, and desires — but don't we all? Failures are just some of life's little experiences. They're tools to grow with and learn from. They aren't given to stop you from moving forward, but rather to inspire you to be strengthened, look ahead with determination, and go on with endurance.

If you learn to love and accept yourself, it becomes much easier to love others and be tolerant of their faults. Your life can be more joyful if you see the good instead of the bad and realize just how beautiful this world is.

Just for today, look at yourself with a heart full of love, understanding, forgiveness, kindness, and gentleness. Remember that you matter enough to have been created by a God who crafted you in His image and designed you to fulfill a purpose that fits into His plans.

You are important to God. Take your experiences and use them to shape better and brighter days ahead.

Cathleen Zeller

God Can Make
All the Difference
in Your Life

To know that God
   is always with you —
that He'll never leave
   or forsake you —
makes all the difference in life.
When hardships come,
sadness arrives,
or plans don't work out —
you aren't alone.
You have God's wisdom
and His special comfort.
He has a better path for you
   to follow.
God isn't worried about
   what to do;
He knows what is best for you.
He makes all things work out
   in the best way
for those who love Him.
And He can make that
   very special difference
      in your life.

Barbara J. Hall

A Morning Prayer
to Fill Your Day
with Peace and Joy

"AS I stand on the edge of this day,
Grant me the strength I need
    to move forward on this journey
      with grace.
Grant me the courage to travel
    with compassion as my companion
      through each hour;
The humor to lighten each moment
    and to bring light and laughter
      to others I meet;
Smiles to scatter along the path
    that stretches before me.

Grant me the wisdom to recognize stones
    on my path and to be able to
       distinguish between
Those I can move, those I can step over,
    and those I need to leave alone.
Grant me the calmness to accept that
    I don't always have to be right,
To face difficulties with serenity,
    and to find peace within myself.
Grant me the skills and confidence
    to face whatever challenges and joys
       this day brings,
And grant me the capacity to relish
    every moment."

Angela M. Churm

Have Faith

Remember that you are a part
    of a limitless love
and you will find strength
    you never imagined.

The combination of your faith
    and God's power
can achieve things beyond
    your wildest dreams.

Allow His love into your soul
and let Him guide you along the path
you were always meant to follow.

Trust that things will turn out
as they were meant to be.
God has brought you this far,
and He will always be
    close by your side.

Jason Blume

On the Road to Your Dreams...

Start each day with praise and a prayer: praise God for your life and thank Him for your blessings. Pray for guidance and good health for others and yourself.

Look at each day as your very own garden. Decide what you want to accomplish. Then sow the right seeds, nurture them appropriately, and believe they'll grow and bloom into the most beautiful flowers you've ever seen.

Don't waste time worrying. Just let your heart and mind lead you to act on your own best advice to yourself. Release the rest. You can only do *your* part and that's enough.

Find something to enjoy in everything you do. If you give joyfully, you are making a deposit in your blessings account, the account that gives back to you what you've sown.

If you love others and treat them as you want to be treated, you are keeping the greatest commandment. And just as you've started each day with praise and a prayer, end the day in the same way. The rest of it will take care of itself.

Donna Fargo

Your Destiny Is in God's Hands

God has created me
to do Him some definite service.
He has committed some work to me
which He has not committed to another.
I have my mission.

I may not know what it is in this life.
But I shall be told in the next.
I am a link in a chain,
a bond of connection between persons.
He has not created me for nothing.
I shall do good. I shall do His work.

Therefore I will trust Him.
Whatever I do, wherever I am, I cannot be
    thrown away.
If I am in sickness, my sickness may serve Him.
If I am in sorrow, my sorrow may serve Him.
He does nothing in vain. He knows what He
    is about.

Cardinal John Henry Newman

Keep Believing in Miracles

Keep believing in the
here-and-now,
down-to-earth, everyday
kind of miracles,
like the first star emerging
in the evening sky,
the sun breaking
through a storm,
and that amazing rainbow
over your world.
Catch a glimpse of heaven
in every person's face.
Keep believing in bright endings,
in giving more than you receive,
and in the overwhelming goodness of people.
See the miracle of each new day
as spectacular and unique
as the sunrise that brings it.

See the miracle of even the tiniest snowflake,
each totally different from another,
just like each of us —
no other like you in the whole world.
Miracles come wrapped in a stranger's smile,
in a kind word just when you need it most,
and, especially, in a friend's hug.
Every time someone makes a difference
in someone else's life,
it's a tiny miracle.
Everyday miracles
are always happening.
Just open your eyes.
You may not have to see it
to believe it,
but you may have to believe it
to see it.

Vickie M. Worsham

God Will Light
Your Path

When the road of life
   seems long and hopeless
Believe you can take the journey
   with God by your side
When the road becomes dark and silent
Believe God will light your way
Believe you have Him with you always
   and keep Him close
When you have God by your side
   life will always be full of hope
   and full of His love for you
He will guide you through
   the trying times of life
   and forgive any mistakes
      along the way
As long as you believe

Deborah Lennox

There's Always
a Way...

God has a thousand ways
Where I can see not one;
When all my means have reached their end
Then His have just begun.

Esther Guyot

Living a life of faith means never knowing
where you are being led. But it does mean
loving and knowing the One who is leading.

Oswald Chambers

Never think that God's delays are God's denials.
Hold on; hold fast; hold out. Patience is genius.

Count de Buffon

When One Door Closes in Our Lives, God Opens Another

Sometimes when we
least expect it,
a door closes in our lives.
Circumstances may change,
dreams may get shattered,
and plans for tomorrow
may disappear.
But when one door closes,
God always opens another.

When we're facing disappointment
    in our lives,
sometimes it's hard to see
that this is also part
    of God's plan —
but it's true.
God knows what is best for us,
and He will lead us
to where we need to be.

Have faith in Him,
and you will reach
all the wondrous things
that He has waiting for you.

B. L. McDaniel

Trust in Yourself
...God Does

Even when times are challenging
and it is difficult to see the positive side,
just remember...

God knows who you are and what
you are made of. He loves you and
encourages you through every twist
and turn you experience, no matter
how subtle His presence may be.

So have faith in yourself. God does,
and He would never place you
anywhere you weren't meant to be.

T. L. Nash

Start Every Day with Prayer

When we know in our hearts that there is a God, the Father of all creation, someone who knows all things and is on our side, it is so natural to want to commune with Him every day... in praise and thankfulness, requesting help and direction for our lives and for those we love.

The repetition of starting each day with prayer helps us decide where we're going, what we want to accomplish, and how we can reach our goals. Prayer quiets our souls, makes us feel centered, and opens the door to getting our needs met. When we look to God as our provider and caregiver, we know we can go to Him boldly with our prayer requests and expect an audience with a compassionate and loving Father. Through our daily prayers, we learn to trust that God wants to supply our needs and give us the desires of our hearts. For what father doesn't want the best for his children?

When others know that we are praying for them in a time of need, it is a comfort to them and, perhaps, the kindest thing we can do for them. When we're trying to resolve a conflict with someone, we may not feel like praying about the situation or for the person involved, but it can be very helpful if we do. Prayer humbles us and softens our sharp edges. It helps us to think more kindly of others and to walk in love. It can not only ease tension and stress to make us feel better, but it can also help generate results for ourselves and for others.

When we speak our words to God with thanksgiving and release them with the faith that our requests will be granted, we put ourselves in a position to receive. God does not change and nature's laws are absolute and impartial. Thus, prayer has the potential for changing us. It connects us with God's spirit, and it is the key to His kingdom. Whatever your religious persuasion, it's a good thing to start every day with prayer.

Donna Fargo

God Will Look After You
One Day at a Time

Life is a continuous experience; but God gives it to us in stages — one day at a time. Anyone who chooses to do so can live one day victoriously. To live each day in this manner is to experience a victorious life.

J. H. Chitwood

Do not look forward to the changes and chances of this life in fear; rather look to them with full hope that, as they arise, God, whose you are, will deliver you out of them. He has kept you hitherto — do you but hold fast to His dear hand, and He will lead you safely through all things; and, when you cannot stand, He will bear you in His arms. Do not look forward to what may happen tomorrow; the same everlasting Father who cares for you today will take care of you tomorrow, and every day. Either He will shield you from suffering, or He will give you unfailing strength to bear it. Be at peace, then, and put aside all anxious thoughts and imaginations.

St. Francis de Sales

Count Your Blessings

Think of the things that make you happy,
Not the things that make you sad;
Think of the fine and true in mankind,
Not its sordid side and bad;
Think of the blessings that surround you,
Not the ones that are denied;
Think of the virtues of your friendships,
Not the weak and faulty side;
Think of the hopes that lie before you,
Not the waste that lies behind;
Think of the treasures you have gathered,
Not the ones you've failed to find;
Think of the service you may render,
Not of serving self alone;
Think of the happiness of others,
And in this you'll find your own!

Robert E. Farley

Your Potential Is Infinite

If seeds in the black earth can turn into such
beautiful roses, what might not the heart of the
human become in its long journey toward the stars?

Gilbert Keith Chesterton

You have the ability
to attain whatever you seek;
within you is every potential
you can imagine.
Always aim higher than
you believe you can reach.
So often, you'll discover
that when your talents
are set free
by your imagination
you can achieve any goal.

Edmund O'Neill

God Loves You Just the Way You Are

He doesn't make mistakes,
and He had a plan when He made you
the beautiful person that you are.

You may not always believe it,
but you are truly special and very important.

It's easy to compare ourselves
to those around us
and to feel as though
we're not good enough.
But God loves all His children,
and each one is in this world for a reason.

Let yourself bask in the warmth of His love,
knowing that He created you
and accepts you as you are.

Jason Blume

God Has Planted a Dream Within You

Deep within our hearts,
God has planted the seed
of a dream that is
special and unique to each one of us.
Sometimes another person
can share that dream
and help it grow to fulfillment;
other times, the dream remains
a solitary pursuit, known only
to the seeker. But secret or shared,
no matter what it might be,
a dream is a potential which
should never be discouraged. For
each of us also carries within ourselves
a God-given light that can cause this seed
to grow and blossom into beautiful reality...
the same light that shines
so clearly in you.

Edmund O'Neill

Make the Most of Your God-Given Talents

What are you going
  to do with your life?
Simply develop yourself;
make the most of the talents
God has given you.
The world needs you
  more than ever before
in a life of effort
that will really count
in the sum of human happiness
  and contentment.

          Frances E. Willard

Have the daring to accept yourself
as a bundle of possibilities, and undertake
the game of making the most of your best.

         Harry Emerson Fosdick

The Answer to Your Prayers

All who call on God in true faith, earnestly from the heart, will certainly be heard, and will receive what they have asked and desired.

Martin Luther

I know not by what methods rare,
But this I know: God answers prayer.
I know not if the blessing sought
Will come in just the guise I thought.
I leave my prayer to Him alone
Whose will is wiser than my own.

Eliza M. Hickok

Prayer must always remain quite ineffective, unless we do everything we can to make our own prayers come true. It is a basic rule of prayer that God will never do for us what we can do for ourselves. Prayer does not do things for us; it enables us to do things for ourselves.

William Barclay

Remember to Give Thanks Along the Way

The art of thanksgiving is *thanksliving*. It is gratitude in action. It is applying Albert Schweitzer's philosophy: "In gratitude for your own good fortune you must render in return some sacrifice of your life for other life."

It is thanking God for the gift of life by living it triumphantly.

It is thanking God for your talents and abilities by accepting them as obligations to be invested for the common good.

It is thanking God for all that men and women have done for you by doing things for others.

It is thanking God for opportunities by accepting them as a challenge to achievement.

It is thanking God for happiness by striving to make others happy.

It is thanking God for beauty by helping to make the world more beautiful.

It is thanking God for inspiration by trying to be an inspiration to others.

It is thanking God for health and strength by the care and reverence you show your body.

It is thanking God for the creative ideas that enrich life by adding your own creative contributions to human progress.

It is thanking God for each new day by living it to the fullest.

It is thanking God by giving hands, arms, legs, and voice to your thankful spirit.

It is adding to your prayers of thanksgiving, acts of *thanksliving*.

Wilferd A. Peterson

God Is
Always Close

God isn't far away.
He is the light of this day.
He is the sky above you,
the earth beneath you,
and the life of every living thing.

He is in every smile,
in every thought that gives you hope,
in every tear that waters your soul,
and in every moment you can't
face alone.

He's the love on your loved one's face.
He's in the friends along the way —
in strangers you have yet to meet
and blessings you have yet to receive.

He's in every good thing
that touches you.
He is in every step you make
and every breath you take.
He's not far away,
for He is with you always.

Nancye Sims

As Long As We Look to the Lord...

We can have hope. Because it works wonders for those who have it. We can be optimistic. Because every cloud does seem to have a silver lining. We can put things in perspective. Because some things are important, and others are not. We can remember that beyond the clouds, the sun is up there shining. We can meet each challenge and give it all we've got.

We can count our blessings. We can be inspired to climb our ladder to the stars. We can be strong and patient. We can be gentle and wise. We can believe in happy endings. Because we are the authors of our stories, we can make them turn out the way we want them to.

We can bring ourselves brighter days.

And we can make our dreams... come true.

Collin McCarty

Hold On to Hope

Hope sees the invisible, feels the
intangible, and achieves the impossible.

Charles Caleb Colton

As long as we have hope, we have direction, the energy
to move, and the map to move by. We have a hundred
alternatives, a thousand paths, and an infinity of dreams.
Hopeful, we are halfway to where we want to go.

Author Unknown

What would this world be without hope? It is the light
in the darkness, joy in sorrow, and strength in weakness;
without it, the world would be desolate indeed. Its beams
are like a great searchlight shining in our hearts, and
brightening up every corner, until we mount, as with
wings, over difficulties and circumstances, and triumph
glorious over the enemy, despair.

Ida Scott Taylor

You Have
a Place
in the Universe

God has a purpose for each one of us, a work for each one to do, a place for each one to fill, an influence for each one to exert... and then, a place for each one to fill in His holy temple.

Arthur C. A. Hall

God is preparing His heroes. And when the opportunity comes, He can fit them into their places in a moment. And the world will wonder where they came from.

A. B. Simpson

Find out what God wants and when you know, try to carry it out cheerfully or at least courageously; not only that, but we must love this will of God and the obligations it entails because whatever God chooses for us, it should be all the same to us.

St. Francis de Sales

Let Faith Guide All Your Steps Through Life

Life has so much to offer. Faith is the key that unlocks the possibilities you have. It opens the door to your potential and uncovers your hidden gifts.

Faith accomplishes great things in small ways. It creates a path through uncharted seas and makes a shoreline so that you may leave your footprints in the sand.

Like a dandelion, faith rises through the cracks in your soul and blossoms. It can work in your life even when you're not aware of it. If you are lacking contentment, if you need direction, or if you're at a loss about what to do — have faith.

Like a seed, let it grow from the tiniest notion to the greatest dream. Once you see the light at the end of the tunnel, you will never walk in darkness again.

You receive life as an uncut rock; within it is a pattern. Chip away what is not part of you, and you will find a purpose just for you. Uncover the truth for yourself, and let faith always guide you.

Tanya P. Shubin

God Is There

Life is a journey
full of twists and turns
and hills and valleys...
but God is there
in every lonely place,
surrounding us with angels,
giving us strength,
offering us hope,
reaching out to us in love
through the prayers
    and good thoughts of others.

May God's love and wisdom
bring you comfort and peace.
May He lead you onward
to greener pastures
and a brighter dawn.
May the love of family
    and friends
be with you forever,
and may God, who is
    always by your side,
help you through everything.

Linda E. Knight

Do Your Best...

We can walk without fear, full of hope and courage and strength... waiting for the endless good which God is always giving as fast as He can get us to take it in.

George MacDonald

He who believes in God is not careful for the morrow, but labors joyfully and with a great heart.... They must work and watch, yet never be careful or anxious, but commit all to Him, and live in serene tranquility; with a quiet heart, as one who sleeps safely and quietly.

Martin Luther

Have courage for the great sorrows of life and patience for the small ones; and when you have laboriously accomplished your daily task, go to sleep in peace. God is awake.

Victor Hugo

and Leave the Rest to God

Find your strength. Search for that smile of yours that makes everything brighter. Hang in there, even though that can be easier said than done. Have faith.

Don't give up. Make a commitment... between your determination, your hopes, and your heart... that your sun *is* going to shine in the sky. Live your life a day at a time, and things will get better by and by.

Find your way through the days with the light that shines within you. Leave a smile where there wasn't one before. Help a hurt; make it mend. Find the strength to make things right again.

Go forward, from one steppingstone to another. Reach out a little farther. If you believe you can, then you *will* make it through. Listen a little more often to what your heart has to say. Do the things that are important to you.

Make today everything you dreamed it could be. Don't settle for less; don't accept what you should not. Use the precious hours you've been given as wisely as you can. Then do your best, and leave the rest to God.

Chris Gallatin

Anything Is Possible Because of God

It is God who enables you
to smile in spite of tears;
to carry on when you feel like giving in;
to pray when you're at a loss for words;
to love even though your heart has been
    broken time and time again.
It is God who enables you
to sit calmly when you feel like throwing
    up your hands in frustration;
to be understanding when nothing
    seems to make sense;
to listen when you'd really rather not hear;
to share your feelings with others
    because sharing is necessary
        to ease the load.

Anything is possible
because God makes it so.

Faye Sweeney

God Has a Plan for Each of Us

And there is such a wonderful plan for you!

May the paths you walk and the roads you travel take you to amazing places. Places where you see the possibilities, where you discover what it's like when dreams come true, and where you come to understand the promise and the potential of all the wonderful qualities inside of you.

May God's plan for you gradually unfold
before your eyes, and — like guiding lights
continually showing the way — may you
find glimmers of hope and happiness
shining every single day.

May the people in your life appreciate what
it's like to be in the presence of someone as
special as you are. You have the kind of gifts
that are given to so few.

God has a plan for each of us...
and may you know there is an especially
    wonderful one... for you.

Alin Austin

Remember His Promise

"I am always with you."
This is the promise of God to one and all —
to every heart that's hurting, grieving,
or burdened with pain.
He offers hope and comfort.
He offers caring and companionship.
He offers peace of mind.
God didn't say the sun would always
    shine on each day.
He didn't say the flowers would
    always bloom.
He didn't say time would always
    bring us perfect happiness.
But God gave humanity a place to go —
a place where peace is always offered,
comfort is always given,
and love is a constant thing.
God said, "I am always with you,"
    and He always is.

Barbara J. Hall

God Knows the Dreams in Your Heart

...and He Will Help Make Them Come True

Believe in yourself.
Remember that with God
all things are possible;
trust in the possibilities
alive within you.
Rise above the storm
until the sun peeks through;
reach out and touch the stars
    within your reach.
Let your spirits rise
as freely as the wind.
Open your heart to miracles,
and follow it all the way
    to your dreams.

Treasure the little thoughts
God plants along your way,
and watch them bloom and grow.
With grace and joy, be
    everything you can be.
Trust completely in God
and know He has great big plans
    for you.
Each step you take is a part
    of life's bigger picture
and part of God's promise
for a better day, a brighter dawn,
and new dreams... just for you.

Linda E. Knight

With Faith in God,
You Can Achieve
Everything You Dream Of

God has blessed you with unique
   talents and abilities; use those gifts well!
Take nothing for granted; rather, work hard
   to prepare for challenges in the future.
Just as important as the lessons that you
   learn along the way are the ways that you
   grow as a person: the friendships you
   form and the deeper understanding you
   acquire of yourself and others.

As you celebrate each milestone in your life
   and look toward new horizons, never
   forget what has brought you this far.
Remember the love of your family and
   friends. Remember your own sacrifice
   and hard work. And remember that God
   has a special plan for your life.
You have so much to be thankful for and so
   much to look forward to!

Pamela Koehlinger

ACKNOWLEDGMENTS

We gratefully acknowledge the permission granted by the following authors and authors' representatives to reprint poems or excerpts from their publications.

Cathleen Zeller for "Just for Today... See Yourself the Same Way God Does." Copyright © 2006 by Cathleen Zeller. All rights reserved.

Barbara J. Hall for "God Can Make All the Difference in Your Life." Copyright © 2006 by Barbara J. Hall. All rights reserved.

Angela M. Churm for "A Morning Prayer to Fill Your Day with Peace and Joy." Copyright © 2006 by Angela M. Churm. All rights reserved.

Jason Blume for "Have Faith" and "God Loves You Just the Way You Are." Copyright © 2006 by Jason Blume. All rights reserved.

PrimaDonna Entertainment Corp. for "On the Road to Your Dreams..." and "Start Every Day with Prayer" by Donna Fargo. Copyright © 2006 by PrimaDonna Entertainment Corp. All rights reserved.

Vickie M. Worsham for "Keep Believing in Miracles." Copyright © 2006 by Vickie M. Worsham. All rights reserved.

Deborah Lennox for "God Will Light Your Path." Copyright © 2006 by Deborah Lennox. All rights reserved.

T. L. Nash for "Trust in Yourself ...God Does." Copyright © 2006 by T. L. Nash. All rights reserved.

Heacock Literary Agency for "Remember to Give Thanks Along the Way" from THE ART OF LIVING by Wilferd A. Peterson, published by Simon & Schuster, Inc. Copyright © 1972 by Wilferd A. Peterson. All rights reserved.

Tanya P. Shubin for "Let Faith Guide All Your Steps Through Life." Copyright © 2006 by Tanya P. Shubin. All rights reserved.

Linda E. Knight for "God Is There" and "God Knows the Dreams in Your Heart." Copyright © 2006 by Linda E. Knight. All rights reserved.

A careful effort has been made to trace the ownership of selections used in this anthology in order to obtain permission to reprint copyrighted material and give proper credit to the copyright owners. If any error or omission has occurred, it is completely inadvertent, and we would like to make corrections in future editions provided that written notification is made to the publisher:

BLUE MOUNTAIN ARTS, INC., P.O. Box 4549, Boulder, Colorado 80306.